The Small Business Handbook
25 Profitable Small Business Ideas

Minute Help Guides

Minute Help Press
www.minutehelp.com

© 2012. All Rights Reserved.

Table of Contents

INTRODUCTION 4
   The First Step: A Foolproof Business Plan 4
   Format 5

CHOOSING A BUSINESS TO START 10
   Franchise Opportunities 10
      SuperGlass Windshield Repair 10
      Tax Service (H&R Block) 12
      Candy Bouquet 13
      RE/MAX LLC 15
   Turn Key Options 17
      Food Vending Machines 17
      DVD Vending 19
   Online Storefront Options 20
      Etsy Store 20
      Ebay Store (Crafts, resell, drop-ship) 22
      Freelance 24
   Professional Options 25
      Paralegal 25
      Payroll, Bookkeeping, Accounting 27
      Security 28
   Direct Sales 29
      Advocare 30
      Thirty-one Gifts 31
   Other Options 33
      Restaurants 33
      Catering 36
      Daycare/ Babysitting (Adults and Children) 37
      Cleaning Services (Home or Office) 39
      Yard/ Outdoor work 41
      Towing Service 43
      Event Planning 44
      Decorating (special events, holidays, interior design) 46
      Computer Repair/ Support 48
      Workshops and Lessons 49
      Pet/ Animal Care or Capture 51

ABOUT MINUTE HELP PRESS..53

Introduction

Going into business for yourself is no small feat. Whether it is a franchise or you go it alone, there are sure to be numerous obstacles along the way. Sometimes the hardest part is getting started. If you already have an idea that you want to bring to life, you are way ahead of the game. If you do not, there are tons of ideas out there just waiting to be had. Seize one and make it your own. Most often when it comes to starting your own small business, you will get out of it exactly what you put into it.

The First Step: A Foolproof Business Plan

Once you know what kind of business you are going to start, it is essential to develop a business plan. This is not only the guideline by which you will run your business, but it is also necessary when seeking funding both for start-up and for future growth. Having a business plan is non-negotiable, but how do you develop and write a business plan that will stand up to even the toughest critics and guide you through good times and bad when it comes to running your business?

Format

Presenting a business plan that is not professionally formatted is unacceptable. It will warrant nothing but a glance, and funding will be out of the question. Even if financing is not an issue, it is still vital to develop a winning business plan and have it written in a professional format. Not only will it be easier for you and others involved to follow, but it will be ready should you need to use it to secure funding in the future. A professional, foolproof business plan should contain the following:

- Cover page

    This may seem to go without saying, but it is alarming how often it is left out. While to some it may seem an unnecessary endeavor, a business plan without a cover page will be tossed by anyone considering it for funding. In fact, it will never make it to the consideration phase.

    A cover page should contain:
    - Business name
    - Address
    - Phone number
    - Owners or executives

If a cover page with these basic elements is not included with a business plan, most serious investors or lenders will not even look at it.

- Table of Contents

   This is a vital piece of a business plan because it makes it more readable. If a potential investor or lender has a specific question, the Table of Contents can help them find exactly where it is discussed in the document. Another way it is used is to get an idea of what information is included in the business plan. Be sure to take note. All business plans should include the same general information, and a quick glance at the contents page can tell an investor whether it is a complete plan or not. If it is not complete, it is dead in the water.

- Executive Summary

   Although it is included just after the Table of Contents, it should be the last portion of the business plan written. It will include an overview of the business plan. It should first answer the question of what exactly it is you plan to do, It should also discuss how much and what type of financing is being sought after and the details of how it will be spent. Lastly, there should be a vision statement. The strongest vision statements answer the questions of where you are going and how you plan to get there as related to the business.

- The Company

    This is where you tell the story of your business. The past, present, and future are all a part of that. Start-ups will not have much to say about the past, but be sure to include information about the evolution of the market you are entering. The big thing here for start-ups is what your business goals are and how you plan to achieve them. It is also good to consider what need or question your business is going to fulfill or answer. You want those reading this to know your plan, and you want to be able to go back to it yourself for guidance in the future.

- The Market

    This is where you highlight any market research you have done. You want to discuss who your target market group is as well as note any others who may potentially have a use for your product or services. Talk about market testing you have done and what the results were. Take note, you need to do market testing. Do surveys, take polls, offer samples or rely on research already done on others. Whatever you find out should be included here. This is also where you would discuss who your competition is and how you plan to compete with them in the market.

- Product or Service

  This is the meat of what you are going to do and where you do your convincing. These are the details of what the business will be, how it will work, and why it will work. What are you going to do? What are you going to sell? How is this business special? Will you offer a warranty? Put any other important information about what you are offering in this section as well.

- Sales and Promotion

  This is the section where you outline your plan, in detail, for getting your product or service to the people. Will you have a website, a store, or both? Do you intend to use telemarketing, direct mailing, online marketing, or a combination? Will you handle public relations yourself or will you hire a PR firm?

- Funding

This section alone should be between 15 and 30 pages. Rest assured if potential investors or lenders make it this far, they will go through this section with a fine toothed comb. This is where you describe your funding plan in depth. Include what funding sources you expect to utilize, how much you hope to obtain from each source, and exactly how that funding will be used. You will also need to detail exactly how you plan to pay back any borrowed funding, and your projected ROI. Financial statements will also be included, but of course for a start-up project these would be pro forma statements.

The purpose of the business plan is two-fold; you want to have a guideline for running your business, but you also need something solid to present to investors and lenders so that they can have faith in what you are doing. Each section of a winning business plan is equally important, and without even one part, the whole thing is weakened.

Choosing a Business to Start

Of course you should go with something that interests you. When your work is related to your passion everything seems to work out better. Here are some ideas to get you started.

Franchise Opportunities

Starting a business can be scary. A franchise can offer support and a plan along with a proven business structure. Some to consider include:

SuperGlass Windshield Repair

Every town, every neighborhood, every area in general has a need for windshield repair. This company was founded in 1993 in Atlanta by David Casey, Bill Costello and Bill Mitchell. With a relatively low startup cost and the ability to run the franchise from home, this is a great opportunity for someone who enjoys working with automobiles.

Startup Cost: as low as $9,910

Total Investment: Anywhere from 9,900 to $31,000 depending on how and where you choose to run it.

The royalties run 4%, and to be considered for a franchise you must first have a net worth of at least $15,000 and $15,000 liquid cash. If you do not already have this, then this amount could be included in start-up costs.

The beauty of any franchise is the support and marketing you have handed to you. If you choose to open a SuperGlass franchise, here are some considerations to make the business "foolproof."

The Market

Look around your specific area and consider what "sub-areas" might be able to best benefit from this service. Of course you hope to draw business from far and wide, but look closely. Is there a factory located down a road that has loose gravel or other prime fodder to brake windshields? If so, market directly to those employees. Is there a company, such as a taxi service or trucking service, that you could repair windshields for at a cheaper price than their regular repairmen? Let them know you are there.

The Difference

Many full service auto shops will repair windshields, but it can take an unnecessarily long amount of time due to other pressing jobs. As a company that offers one service alone, windshield repair, you can offer a more streamlined experience. Focus on this with your target audience.

The Competition

Scope out the competition, but remember that the competition is not only those full service auto shops. Any business offering windshield repair would be considered competition. This includes other exclusive windshield businesses. You will have to find how you can offer customers something they cannot. Will it be working on site, or maybe offering a cleaner, faster service? Whatever it is, do it and do it well.

Tax Service (H&R Block)

Startup: $2,500 franchise fee plus cost of office space and equipment

In the 1950s the Block brothers founded what some believe has become an American icon. H&R Block is nationally known as one of the most well respected tax services around. It is possible to start a franchise for as little as $31,500, depending on available office space and other variables. The great thing about franchising when it comes to tax services is that even with no formal accounting training, you have the well-respected name and training of H&R Block behind you.

The franchise fee is relatively small, at $2,500, but the royalties are 30%. That being said, if the demand exists, there is plenty to be made. In a large enough area it is possible to own even more than one. The key is to make yourself accessible to everyone. If that means to you set up a kiosk or table away from the office to make yourself more accessible, then so be it. Customer service and great employees are key with this type of business. Training is completely taken care of by H&R Block, and a good portion of advertising is handled as well.

Find a way to get to those who cannot get to you, and do a great job for them. The vast majority of the work is done from January to April, with extensions being handled until October. Use the down time to advertise, and sometimes it is even possible to run a skeleton crew or shut down the office completely out of season. Community involvement is another big factor with this type of business. Support sports teams, charities, and get your name out as much as possible during down times and in the months leading up to tax season.

Candy Bouquet

Startup cost: varies starting at $12,500

Candy Bouquet was started in Barbara McIntyre's Little Rock, Arkansas garage in 1989. She saw a vision of using candy and cookies in arrangements in place of flowers, thinking arrangements should taste good as well as look pretty. Flowers die, but candy and cookies can bring happiness in more than just being observed. In 1993 she began franchising, and now the company boasts units in 49 states, 44 countries, and includes store front as well as home-based versions of the franchise opportunities.

The franchise fee is $7,000 to $35,000 and start-up ranges from $12,470 to $49,350 depending on the franchise option taken. New franchisees are trained at headquarters for five days, and then supported with advertising materials, emails, and newsletters thereafter.

This is ideal for those who love to make beautiful things, enjoy arranging items to make them look their best, or have a knack for decorating. To make this business foolproof, be sure you choose the initial plan that is right for you. If you are going to choose the home-based option, be sure your home space can handle it. If you are going to start out with a store front, be certain that the cost and the location are beneficial to the business. Poor location or rent that is too high can sink a business before it ever starts.

Make it special by emphasizing to the market why Candy Bouquet is better than flowers. Ensure that all of your products, those for special events and specific ages or categories, are being talked about as well as the general population products. Everyone needs to send a quick and easy gift now and then, and if there is no one else offering the service, Candy Bouquet has proven to be an outstanding endeavor for many.

RE/MAX LLC

Startup cost: Varies starting at $35,000

RE/MAX was founded in Denver by Dave and Gail Liniger in 1973. Today it is a global network of real estate agents weighing in at over 116,000. They designed the company in such a way as to offer higher commissions to agents. As such, agents are in charge of their own business and office expenses are shared equally with other agents. All agents operate under a maximum commissions plan.

This business can be started for a minimum of $35,000 total investment. The franchise fees run from $12,500 to $28,000, and the royalties vary. The initial training is fast at only 5 days. However, there will be a significantly longer time investment early on if you are not already a licensed real estate agent.

Real Estate has its highs and lows, so how do you ensure a business such as this will survive the lows? The key is diversity of property. You want plenty of high end, huge income producing property, but you have to have some properties that customers can afford when times are tough. Consider branching out into rentals and property management as well, as the income streams provided by these sources can fill in the gaps between the big sales. Also, remember you can show homes that are not listed with you, though you will not make as much. Be sure to market to buyers as well as sellers. It is also important to do your best to make sure sellers understand how to have their homes ready to sell. Offer pointers on curb appeal, improvements that should be made, and preparing the home for showing to potential buyers. Buyers and sellers make or break a real estate business equally, and it is important to give them both equal attention.

Lastly, you have to get them to come to you. Make yourself visible in the community, and make yourself available. The vast majority of those looking to buy a home or rent a home begin online now. Make sure your listings are on the online hot spots along with how to get in touch with you for more info. Also, be responsive. Respond to email and phone inquiries. You never know when that email or phone call might be the big sale.

Turn Key Options

These refer to many different options. Various types of vending machines and coin machines are the most popular.

Food Vending Machines

Startup Cost: From $500 to $20,000

Vending machines are a time honored tradition. They are a fast, easy solution to a problem we all face at some point in our lives. If we are hungry, thirsty, or just want a snack, then we are likely to get it wherever we can, and vending machines are often the only available option. While there are many possibilities, those that offer food or drink in high traffic areas where there is not another food source are the most successful. Think of office buildings during non-meal times and hospitals after the cafeteria is closed. These are all places where there are people that may get hungry and have no other option but vending.

Prices on vending machines and inventory vary, but there are plenty of options in the less than $50,000 range. The way to make this business plan foolproof without the funds to buy enough machines to make a significant income eventually is to work them on the side. Buy one and place it strategically in a place that positions it for success. Do not rely on it for income right away, but rather keep saving and working until you can buy another, and another, and so on.

Another key to great success in this business is to consider the changing market. There is a health conscious revolution that is not embraced by traditional vending fare, and the government has also jumped on board. The future of vending is in healthy snacks and beverages, and right now there is opportunity to be the first to offer this in many venues. In some venues, including the office building and hospital examples, healthy entrée vending may also be well accepted.

One option for this type of vending is HealhtyYOU vending. Initial investments begin at $20,000, and the only time put in during the beginning stages is the time it takes to get your machines installed. This company also offers remote management of machines, meaning debit and credit funds can be managed online, as well as product rotation and pricing.

There are many options when it comes to vending, but one trap many fall into that can cause failure is the belief that this type of business requires minimal amounts of actual work. This is simply not true. Machines break and have to be repaired, they take money and people want refunds, paper money and change has to be collected and stocked, and product has to be rotated. Work has to be done, but if it is done well, the payoff can eventually exceed the amount of work required greatly.

DVD Vending

Start-up Cost: Starting at $2,000

DVD Vending offers a more convenient, cheaper alternative to the video store. Games and movies can be rented at the kiosk, and the prices are much less than other options for this type of service.

Standard storefront video rental businesses have all but become extinct due to this one revolution. You see these machines in grocery stores, outside of drug stores, and in very close capacity with popular fast food restaurants. They generally start at around $2,000, and again, the only time investment in the beginning is the time to have the machine installed. That is if you do not buy one that is already in place.

Two great things about these types of vending machines is that people will keep coming back because there is something new they want, like a new movie or game, and they can be right across the street from another machine exactly like it and still get business. This is because those who frequent whatever area your machine is at will use your conveniently placed one. They virtually all get business, and often one will get business over another simply because of what DVDs are in stock.

There are always issues of course. Owners are responsible for renting the space for the machine, maintenance, and lost or broken DVDs. A properly placed machine however, will more than pay for these types of incidentals.

Online Storefront Options

Etsy Store

Startup: Variable, less than $500

Etsy is an online market place for selling homemade goods. Anything you make yourself can be sold on Etsy, from baked goods to hair bows, and even electronic printables. Startup costs can be as little as $.20 plus the cost of materials and labor to make your product. Etsy does not charge membership fees, meaning your virtual storefront is free. This is an amazing deal considering customers can pay electronically right on your site, and you do not have to worry about hosting fees, domain names, etc.

They do charge $.20 to post one item for one month, and then they take a 3.5% cut when the item sells. The only time investment is the time is takes to actually make your products and get them listed, and then shipping if that is required.

So in a world full of monogramed baby items, hair bows, and handmade jewelry, how do you make your product successful? The first step is developing a unique product. It does not have to be totally unique, but something about your product has to stand out among all of the rest. Hair bows should have a twist or design that is not available easily anywhere else, baked goods should be unique recipes or a new craze, and if you can come up with something that no one else has you are even better off.

Even if there are a thousand products just like yours, you can build big business with some simple marketing strategies. Utilize social media to get the word out, and take your business on the road to craft fairs and such if the shoe fits. Each of these will get your product in front of your target audience and help you gain a following, which results in sales.

When it comes to social media marketing, you can target groups and networks that cater to your target market. In the hair bow example, you might join moms' groups and groups that buy, sell, and swap children's clothing on Facebook. If you offer organizational printables, you might join groups of people trying to get more organized. There are groups for everything in the social media world. Find those that are relevant and get plugged in.

Ebay Store (Crafts, resell, drop-ship)

Startup: No more than $299/ year for the highest priced store option.

Another online store front option is EBay. It is not for simply selling random items occasionally. It can actually become quite a business if you go about it the right way. While it began as an online auction site, it has evolved to being that and much more. You can offer a set price rather than offering an item for bid, and you can create your own virtual Ebay "store" with its own name and featuring your products.

Products can range from homemade to drop shipping, and even resell. Many have been successful scouring yard sales and flea markets for treasures priced at much less than what they are worth, and then reselling them on Ebay. This is true of jewelry and collectibles as well as high quality, brand name clothing. Of course that is part of overhead, but depending on what you decide to sell overhead could easily be minimal. Consider the fact also that the business is run online, and many already have access to the internet and a computer, equipment and office space costs are virtually non-existent. With the exception of drop shipping, storing products before they ship can be an issue, but it is easy enough to find garage space or a nook in a closet or under a bed.

Consider carefully the cost versus the benefit of certain hidden extras such as insurance on items shipped and the potential to need to add extra storage if business really takes off. The key to making this foolproof is to research what items sell well on the platform and determine which of these you could logically use as a business catalyst. If you love spending time in flea markets, thrift stores, and at yard sales, then that route is for you, but remember to do your research and it is best to have a plan as to what you are looking for. If you know that plus size pants in particular brands do well on Ebay, then you can focus on finding those treasures. If you are better at coordinating and advertising, then a drop shipping option may be best.

Freelance

Startup- variable under $2,000

The sky is virtually the limit here. You can make it as low cost or costly as you want, and you can do basically whatever you choose. The most common freelance jobs of late are content writing, web design, virtual assisting, and accounting or bookkeeping services.

Startup costs vary based on what service you are offering and what equipment you need to make it work. If you are doing web design or accounting, you may need to invest in software. Writing and virtual assisting may not need anything other than a computer, and transcribing will likely need some sort of headset for listening to audio files for transcribing.

The time investment it slightly more than some other options, as getting the news of your service out there can take a bit. Sign up with freelancer groups and keep an eye on the freelance job boards such as Elance and vWorker among others. Some of these charge a fee to bid on jobs, but it is usually reasonable. Also, consider starting your own website to advertise your business, let potential clients see what you have to offer, and even accept payment through. The cost of a domain name and hosting is typically well less than $500 per year.

The best way to make this type of business foolproof it to make sure you are good at and properly trained for whatever service you offer. It is wise to do some pro bono or very cheap work in the beginning to build not only a portfolio but also references. Next, make a commitment to customer service, being certain to do your best to make sure each and every client is happy with your work. Combine that with the availability of freelancer groups and forums online, and word will spread of the great work you do and you will be successful. Be sure to have backup and a budget however, as anyone living the lifestyle will tell you that a freelancer's life is feast or famine.

Professional Options

If you have professional training you can generally strike out on your own whenever you wish. Whether you are a CPA, an attorney, or a paralegal, you have the training part handled already.

Paralegal

This is a business you can really make your own. Many do not realize it is an option to own a paralegal business, but basically rather than working for one specific law firm, you do work for several smaller firms. You can work in their office or your own, and you can even eventually hire employees with the same skills so that you can take on more business.

Startup Cost: variable depending on notary and insurance fees, office space, and employees, but generally less than $30, 000.

To be successful at this, you really have to build a reputation on your own. If you are already working as a paralegal, use your previous employee as a reference if possible. You can also use them for referrals if you are still going to do occasional work for them. If you are not already trained, there are multiple programs that offer paralegal training in a relatively short period of time, but this of course adds to startup costs.

One great way to put a twist on this type of business is to market yourself to local firms as a solution for overflow. Many firms have times when the work volume is too much for the paralegals on staff, and you could be a great relief for that type of situation. If you had enough clients, this could allow you to stay busy, be successful, and maintain flexibility when it comes to schedule and workload.

Payroll, Bookkeeping, Accounting

Startup Cost: less than $500

This is another area where if you are not formally trained, you can become trained fairly quickly and with much less cost than a four year degree would warrant. There are plenty of certificate programs that train in tax preparation and bookkeeping services. Of course if you are an accountant or CPA already you have an advantage, and you may also be able to bring clients from your previous work experience over to your new endeavor.

Startup costs and initial time investment are variable based on many factors. For example, if you have no training, you will have to take classes of some sort, if you do not have a computer or accounting software you will have to invest in that, but if you already have these things you can start for virtually nothing. Many do this type of work from their home, and that even reduces the cost of office space.

To make this foolproof, you will need to be sure you are charging an appropriate rate for each service. Do some research to determine what reasonable hourly rates and flat fees would be for specific services. Also, some bookkeepers charge by transaction. Once you have a set fee, start looking for clients. Think about how the services you offer will be better than the same services offered by others. Do you offer more personalized customer services? Will you handle certain aspects that others will not such as bank deposits or bill paying? If you already have some clients coming over from a previous job, ask for referrals.

It is wise also to check into insurance and bonding prices. Though these will definitely add to overhead costs, it is a small price to pay to be covered when you need to be. One unhappy client or mistake can sink this type of ship, so be aware, do your best, and keep yourself insured.

Security

If you live in a wealthy area, you can work as a personal security guard. You may have only one client or you may work different hours or days for different clients. You can work only during your client's vacation times or other times when they are away, or you can hire others to work with you and run 24-hour shifts. This works especially well for someone who has a military or police training background.

Startup Cost- Less than $500

The only real startup cost is advertising and a uniform. You definitely want a uniform in this type of work as it demands respect. Market any skills you have that would be useful in this type of endeavor, and be sure you are licensed to use any firearm or other weapon you may wield.

Market to those who can both afford and have a use for the services you offer. You may drive rounds through neighborhoods watching for suspicious activity and pay special attention to client's homes, or you may sit vigil while a client works at night. There are those will to pay big money to ensure that a real person is watching out for their loved ones and their belongings.

This is not a business for someone who is not properly trained. Be sure you understand all of the legal aspects of the business, and know when to simply pick up the phone and call the cops. If you do a good and job and are located in the right market, you can make a lucrative career out of this type of business.

Direct Sales

There are mixed feelings about direct sales, but they can be profitable if you find a product you believe in and can afford to make the investment that it takes. The problems come when those involved do not treat it like a business, choose a business in which the market is flooded, or simply give up too soon.

Advocare

Advocare is a direct sales company specializing in health and wellness products. They offer weight loss products, dietary supplements, and a few beauty products.

Startup Cost: as low as $79

The beauty of Advocare is that the products are both high quality and consumable. This means that those who start using them often come back for more. The high volume of repeat customers is one reason why so many see great success in the business. Another reason is the relatively low saturation of distributors in relation to the market saturation of many other direct sales businesses. Mary Kay and Avon are everywhere, but Advocare is much more scarce. It is growing however, so now is the time to jump in if sales is your thing.

With the minimum investment of $79 you earn 20% of all sales. As your sales volume increases you earn more, and unlike other similar companies, there is no quota ever. Once you hit $3,000 in sales over 3 consecutive pay periods you are promoted to advisor and eligible for other types of payment. You can also pay $3,000 at sign up and pay right in to advisor. This warrants you $3,000 worth of product, and you have the opportunity to make it all back plus some when the inventory is sold.

You never have to keep inventory on hand, and in fact it is discouraged. There are multiple opportunities for training, which are not required but deemed very helpful by the company. While it is a standard pyramid sales organizational strategy, there are many who are very successful. To make it foolproof, try the products first and fall in love with them yourself. If you do this, you will not have to sell, only tell. Next, follow the advice of those there before you. They got where they are for a reason, and they are usually willing to help get you there too. They are well rewarded when they do.

In addition to selling face to face, you are provided a microsite through which orders can be placed directly by customers.

Thirty-one Gifts

This is another relative newbie in the direct sales world. The products include mostly various types of bags and organizational tools in fun patterns. These include utility totes, picnic equipment, lunch bags, and even wallets and coupon organizers.

Startup Cost: $99

This is a standard pyramid party organizational plan, but is much less well known than others. This along with the product variety makes it a somewhat more successful endeavor if you are interested. Be aware however, that you must be 100% committed to it, and you must have at least $200 in sales over 3 consecutive months. This can be your own purchases, but that does not earn enough profit to consider this a business.

To be successful, get out there. Get a booth at every vendor fair, join every possible group related to the target market, donate product to giveaways and auctions, and get your name out in the community. You can also do catalog parties that do not require the host to have people in their homes, and you are provided with a micro site that orders can be placed through as well.

Direct sales have a whole new friend on the internet these days. It is now possible to reach more people than ever before, and it is easier and more convenient for customers as well. Set up a Facebook page for your products and be sure to get the link to your micro site out there for everyone to see.

These are not consumable products, meaning that there is not that draw to keep customers coming back. The best angle to work here is every woman's desire for organization, and the need for unique gifts. These items can be personalized and given at wedding showers and baby showers as well as for Christmas and for birthdays. Ramp up marketing efforts during the holidays, around June when weddings are especially popular, and make yourself accessible for those needing last minute gifts. Pair all of this with excellent customer service, showing how your product can meet each individual's needs, and you have a recipe for success.

Other Options

Restaurants

Opening a restaurant is something that is very risky, but with the right plan it can also be very successful. There are tons of things that have to be considered from what type of establishment you want to run, what kind of food you want to serve, and where you are going to order your food from. You have to hire employees for serving and cooking, and you have to pass health department inspections and fire code regulations. Still, in the end if you handle things properly you can be successful.

Startup Cost: variable but possible for less than $50,000

If you simply find a building and start cooking it is likely you are not going to be very successful. If you want to open a restaurant, you need to find a market that you can compete in and keep it simple. Let growth of capacity and menu come slowly. The best angle to get started is to concentrate on cleanliness, customer service, and great food. Lack of variety on the menu and lack of sitting room are much more easily forgivable than poor service, unsanitary conditions, or nasty food. Location is also important. If you set up where you are highly visible, or if you are an option to those who previously had no options, you are half way there.

If you are trying to keep costs down, do so by choosing a smaller building for less money, and limit menu variety. If there are only fast food burger joints in town, open a diner offering homemade burgers and maybe an option for a hot dog or chicken strips for those who may not be up for a burger. Concentrate on only one or two sides such as fries and onion rings, and focus on making those offerings the best available. Advertise and offer incentives to get people in during a grand opening, and once they taste what you have they will be back. Increase variety by offering extra add on options such as chili, cheese, and relish that can be used on most any of the staple menu items.

Once you start to grow, a business like this can add items such as a BLT that uses items already on hand for burgers, and even grilled cheese sandwiches. Later on add fish dinners or meat and three options if business is good, but in the beginning just stick to the basics and make those really, really good.

Of course there are other restaurant options. Mexican, Asian, seafood, pizza, Italian, and virtually any other kind of food you want to offer. Pizza is a great option if you want to be creative as there are an unlimited number of pizza possibilities. If you are good, people will come back because they cannot get what you are serving anywhere else. The more complicated you get the more money you are going to have to spend, so if you do not have your heart set on something elaborate, keep the restaurant business small, simple, and clean in the beginning to have a better shot at success.

Catering

This is similar to a restaurant business, but a little easier to run in some ways. Be careful as some licensing requirements demand an industrial kitchen for food preparation. This could add to startup costs.

Startup costs: Around $20,000 depending on cost of kitchen upgrades and equipment, including a van if needed to haul food.

In truth the most expensive part of getting this business started is the cost of kitchen upgrades. Build up slowly though by simply helping family and friends with food for events. You can charge costs plus a small percentage for labor, and worry about kitchen upgrades, licensing and insurance, and better travel arrangements as the business grows. Getting started, buy some used buffet equipment to keep food warm, and simply carry everything in the vehicle you already have.

Word of mouth is the best form of marketing for this kind of business. Keep cards ready and available, and get your name out in other ways as well. Far and away however you will find that word of mouth is what will bring in the most business. Do events for free or very low cost starting off, offer samples at vendor fairs, and keep cards on you at every single event you cater.

If you are particularly great at something specific, you can limit yourself to a business providing just that one thing. For example, if you make great homemade bread or bread products, get the word out that you will make bread, rolls, or whatever you want for special events. You can find those customers that want your services weekly, and you will have plenty of repeat customers during the holiday season. The same thing works for cookies, cupcakes, or even pies. Give out samples and let the word spread about how delicious your offerings are. Put an ad in the paper as well as on public forums. Never miss an opportunity to get your product in the public. If you take something to a party, take something you would sell and place a card nearby. If you bake a cake for a party, whether you are paid or not, leave enough cards for all the guests so they can order their own.

Starting any type of food service business is risky, so be certain you understand all of the safety and liability rules before you get started. One case of food poisoning could shut you down for good.

Daycare/ Babysitting (Adults and Children)

Startup cost: Virtually nothing

One of the most common small businesses to run is a daycare center. For children, it is easy to do this from your own home. If you are looking at running an adult daycare service it may have to be done differently. Either way you go, these services are always needed, and there is always a market for dependable, loving caregivers.

It is very common for daycare businesses to be run out of private homes. If there is a lack of good, dependable childcare services in your area then you already have a leg up. Remember, however, that parents will not leave their children with just anyone. You will need people willing to be a reference for you. You will also have to decide what all your services will include. Will you provide lunch? Will they need to bring their own nap time bedding? What hours will you run? To be truly successful offer as much as possible for as little as possible without making yourself lose money. If you can provide healthy snacks and a nutritious lunch in a loving environment, you will likely have to turn people away. To offer a really unique service and virtually guarantee success, offer all of this on a 24 hour basis. Overnight childcare is very difficult to find and needed more often than is realized.

To go a different route, consider offering yourself as an adult caregiver. This service is not one that would run out of your home, but rather you would offer yourself to sit with adults who need constant care while their regular caregiver has a break. Children caring for elderly parents often need to run errands or just need a break without their charge with them. Even those who already have hired help have need for backup due to illness or other situations that keep their help from being there. You may sit for several hours each day or for only a couple of hours each week. Build up a clientele and you could become very busy very quickly.

A word of caution however; if you do not have medical skills make sure clients know this. If you are simply going to sit and keep them company while making yourself available to get help if needed, that is fine. Just be sure no one expects that you can handle nursing responsibilities if you cannot.

Cleaning Services (Home or Office)

Another very popular and low overhead startup small business is a cleaning service. Offer your services to clean private homes or offices for those that will pay you to do it for them. Be warned that if you work for offices it may require nights and weekend due to not being able to work during hours when employees are there, but business clients tend to pay more as well.

Startup costs: around $300

Startup costs include the costs of supplies and cleaning materials, and this is of course variable. If you start out slow some of these costs can be deferred until your business grows. Start by getting your name out and finding a few clients willing to give you a shot. Advertise in local papers and with flyers, and be sure you have plenty of cards lying around town for those who are interested. When it comes to businesses, go to them personally and deliver a card and quote for services.

Though you can require your clients to supply cleaning materials, to really offer a successful service handle your own supplies. To start, they simply have to work. As you grow, you can invest in more professional cleaning supplies. Another way to increase your likelihood of success is to become bonded. This adds cost, but goes a long way toward gathering clients.

This is probably one of the easiest businesses to start. If you can do a great job in a short amount of time you can build quite a decent business that pays very well. The better you are the more clients you will have interested, and the faster you are the more clients you will be able to take on. Remember that word of mouth plays a vital role in this industry as well. If you hire others to work with you ensure they are completely trustworthy. One stolen item or poor job is all it takes to stop the business before it ever gets started.

Even if you offer your own supplies, be willing to be flexible. Some people have allergies to certain products, or even just preferences for their own products. Be willing to use them if they are willing to provide. Also, be very clear about your "menu" of services. It can be helpful to have a list of basic services for a set price, and then a list of add-on services for an additional price. For example, basic cleaning such as floors, dusting, appliances, and bathrooms may be $100 per visit, and then they can add windows, baseboards, closet organization, or laundry services each for an additional price.

Start slow with one or two clients to get your name out there and build up a good reputation, and you could have a very successful cleaning business very quickly.

Yard/ Outdoor work

The work involved in this type of business is seasonal to a large extent, but it can be very lucrative despite its non-consistent nature. This is more than grass cutting. In the summer you can keep very busy. But if you add in storm cleanup, gutter cleaning, and landscaping, you can keep a more steady flow of work than you might expect.

Startup Costs: Between $20,000 and $30,000 depending on necessary equipment for services offered.

If you offer all of the above listed services, you will need ladders, limb cutting equipment, safety attire, lawn mowers, weed eaters, you get the point. If all of that is not feasible immediately, start with a ladder, a lawn mower, and a weed eater. You can get started quite nicely with this. You will need a truck and trailer for hauling the mower and downed limbs if you are doing storm cleanup. In the fall, you can stay busy with a rake and a leaf blower, and invest in a snow shovel or snow blower if you live in an area that gets significant snow, and you have yourself a steady business. In the winter time ice and snow storms can cause storm damage as well, which is another opportunity to offer your services.

You can choose from a gamut of landscaping services, but something simple like pulling weeds, adding mulch, and trimming hedges fits well with this type of service. If you wish to get into more detailed landscaping endeavors it will likely take special training and cut into your time to do the other list of services already mentioned. Keeping things simple and slow is the best way to build a successful business with little money upfront.

As your business grows, you can add equipment and employees, which will allow you to take on more clients and grow even more. This is the kind of business that is best to build slowly, one step at a time. You are filling a need, and it is hard work. There are not many that are willing to do the kind of backbreaking work that this entails, which puts you at an advantage from the start. If you are willing and do a great job, you are likely to be very successful at this business.

Towing Service

If you have a tow truck, you can make a substantial amount of money towing people. The more trucks and drivers you have the more you can make, but just a one man show is all that is needed to get a business such as this off of its feet.

Startup Cost: The cost of a tow truck and insurance, around $30,000 depending on whether your rent, or buy new or used.

This is a business that can be run straight from your home. It is nothing more than having the truck and being available to take the call when it comes in. The need to be available at all hours is the major drawback with this type of business. The hours are not really set. You would need to be available at all times with few exceptions, which means sticking as close to your area as possible and being available even during the wee hours of the morning.

Of course to be successful, you have to be sure those who need your services know that you offer them and choose you as their provider. The most effective way to do this is to be certain your information is in all of the phone listings, and if you have an ad in the yellow pages be sure your available hours are listed. Another great way to gain business is to partner with local mechanics. If someone calls a mechanic and needs a tow, it would be great to be the one he recommends.

While all areas need a tow truck at some time or another, this type of business can be especially profitable if you live near an interstate and are willing to cover a sizeable area. While competition could become an issue in a smaller town, a metropolitan area or even a smaller town on an interstate is going to have a much greater demand for towing services.

Consider beforehand the areas you will cover, and if it involves nearby towns. Work with the mechanics there, too. You can work out deals where they get a cut of your fee for recommendation, or better yet allow them to advertise themselves as a repair *and* tow service and contract the towing part out to you.

Event Planning

Event planners handle all of the details for various types of events from birthday and anniversary parties to weddings and Bar Mitzvahs. **For those talented individuals who can do this type of work, a business such as this can be very rewarding and profitable.**

Startup Cost: Only what you can spend on marketing

As an event planner, you would do the leg work of finding a venue, ordering and scheduling food, flowers, other decorations, the guest list, invitations, etc. You will not cook the food, put out the decorations, or do anything else hands on. You simply organize and schedule everything so that the client only has to show up to a party that is perfectly planned to their specifications.

Be warned, while it sounds easy it takes a love of organization and stellar customer service to be successful. It also helps to be resourceful and careful with the client's budget. Don't go for broke, but rather show them that you can get them what that want at the best price possible.

This is another one that needs to start with doing some free or cheap business for a few to get your name out, and be sure to list your services on every possible platform. Forge relationships and even partnerships with local florists, caterers, bakeries, and decoration rental companies. Work with them closely and you are more likely to be the one who gets the deals, gets the results, and thus gets the clients. Leave contact information at these businesses as well, as there may be someone there just fed up enough of doing it themselves to be ready to call you in.

The more stress you take off the client, the better. The most successful event planners know what to ask in the first meeting to get started and basically leave them alone until pertinent decisions have to be made. Be careful to keep all costs organized and ready to answer budget related questions at any minute. If you are effective and efficient you will be hired again and again.

Decorating (special events, holidays, interior design)

Those with a flair for decorating can market their services as an interior designer. This can include entire homes, single rooms, and even seasonal décor. It is amazing the people who are willing to hire someone to hang pictures tastefully, arrange their furniture, and decorate a Christmas tree. If these are things you are exceptionally good at then this type of business could be for you.

Startup Cost: only marketing costs

This is the type of job where you only have to show up and do the work. If you are responsible for purchasing décor you are given a budget by the client and you go shop for them. You use what they make available, create something beautiful, and get paid for doing it. So how do you make this type of business foolproof? It is all in the network. Of course first you have to be good at what you do, and there needs to be clients who will back that up. Find family and friends who will let you do their homes and create a portfolio of pictures so potential clients and networking partners can see samples of your work.

Those necessary to include in a network to be successful in this type of business include realtors, furniture store owners, art galleries, florists, and pretty much anyone owning any type of retail business that deals in home décor. When customers buy from them they may mention in passing that they are moving and need someone to decorate, and your name can be recommended. Realtors can suggest you to those trying to sell their home to set up staging. It is amazing how a network can really drum up business.

When the seasons change and everyone is decorating for the fall or winter holidays or seasons, get the word out that you can make their home beautiful for the season. Put an ad in the paper, and if you can get permission to use a picture from a past client, include it. This is especially useful if you are great at doing unique and beautiful Christmas trees, mantels, or other specific scenes. Show off what you can do and watch them come running.

During this time of year, you can add Christmas tree farms to your networking list as well. If they are not interested in a partnership you can ask permission to leave contact information or even flyers with pictures of trees done previously for those buying trees to see. The important thing to remember when running this type of business is that you have to keep your creativity in line with the client's budget. They want you to do the best you can inside their financial parameters. The more creative you get with where you shop and what you use, the better.

Computer Repair/ Support

With the amazing advances in technology coming through every day, the need for computer repair and support is growing by leaps and bounds. If you are qualified to do this it is almost a sure thing that you will have plenty of business.

Startup Costs: Whatever it costs you to rent office space and for any needed tools; less than $20,000.

More and more companies are outsourcing computer support overseas, and more and more customers are becoming frustrated with the practice. Many times technicians are difficult to understand and condescending. If you can offer the same service with a great attitude, you are likely to make a great success out of this type of business.

To make this situation foolproof, do not focus on individuals alone. There is definitely a market for working on the computers of individuals, but it is unlikely it will be enough to float the business at first. To really get the business up and running, find out who local businesses use for their computer repair needs, learn what it will take to compete, and go get contracts. You can offer your services a la carte or you can work on retainer. Either way, if you can land a couple of contracts and keep some private work to fill in the gaps, this can be a very lucrative business.

Keep in mind that while individuals may bring their machines to you and may even be willing to leave them for a short time, businesses will not be so flexible. When they are without computers they will want them up and running as quickly as possible and with as little interruption as possible. This means getting in, figuring out what it wrong, fixing it, and getting out. You have to be willing to offer stellar customer service to maintain these contracts, and without fail these contracts are needed, at least a couple of them, to stay successful.

Workshops and Lessons

If you have a special skill, you can offer workshops and training courses to teach these skills to others interested in learning them.

Startup cost: $2,000 to $3,000 depending on venue costs for classes and materials needed for students.

The sky is really the limit here. If you played sports in high school or college, you can offer to do workshops for children to help them excel at the sport. If you were a cheerleader you could offer private lessons or workshops. If you are an excel guru or couponista, you can offer workshops to those who want to learn more, and there are always the old standbys of piano lessons or swimming lessons.

If you have good material and are a great teacher, this can be lucrative. You do need to verify demand for the lessons you want to teach, and a lot of that will depend on where you are located. If there is a large market for private lessons you can go strictly that route. Pretty much anything you are really good at can become a money maker however. Even teaching workshops about scrapbooking, wreath making, how to save money, or any combination. You simply have to advertise for students and get a place to have the class. Cooking lessons are even an option.

If you choose to do this as a business, there are some things to consider. First, you will have to be able to charge enough to make a profit, so if you are doing crafts or something else that requires materials you will need to take those costs into consideration when setting a fee. Also realize that you will have to hold classes or workshops during times when students can attend. This will likely result in your main working hours being during the evenings and on weekends.

Pet/ Animal Care or Capture

There is an amazing demand for animal catching. Crazy things get into homes, and the everyday Joe cannot get them out themselves. If you have a raccoon in your attic, a bird in your fire place, or a snake under your bed you want it gone and gone now. A "critter getter" type of business can be very profitable.

Startup Cost: Marketing cost and cost of protective attire

This is a tricky one because you really do have to be careful. However, the danger factor is the reason why people are willing to pay good money for it. As long as you have protective gear and proceed with caution, you are fine. Most would not consider starting this type of business without being qualified.

If you know of an area that has a lot of wildlife, such as a subdivision near a heavily wooded area, it can be helpful to leave flyers on doors or cars in those neighborhoods. Make sure to let it be known that you are there for the safety of everyone, including the animal.

The key to success here is to get the word out. The service is unique because you offer quick response time and animal safety. This is the type of business where radio and television ads getting this information out are ideal. You can also increase your service base by trying to find hurt or lost pets. Be careful to get the point across however that finding pets are not the main gig. Birds fly into dryer vents and get stuck in houses, squirrels run into the garage and get lost, snakes crawl in when no one is looking and curl up under the sink. These are what people really need help with, and if you offer a service that will come in, safely remove the animals, and get them to a safe place, you are going to be in demand.

Whatever type of business you choose to start, the keys to success are marketing and quality product. If you get the word out and do what you do well, the business will do fine assuming you did the necessary research to ensure the demand was there. Be prepared for a slow start. Lasting success does not come over night, but if you have a solid business plan and a great product or service, success will come. When you feel discouraged, refer back to your business plan and stay on task. If you have backup funding, as you always should, you have a little wiggle room. If you are not getting business, ramp up the marketing scheme, and if you are not getting repeat business, look closely at what customers are saying. Make any necessary adjustments, and keep your nose to the grindstone. Owning your own business is possible, it is rewarding, but it is not easy.

About Minute Help Press

Minute Help Press is building a library of books for people with only minutes to spare. Follow @minutehelp on Twitter to receive the latest information about free and paid publications from Minute Help Press, or visit minutehelp.com.

Cover image © mangostock - Fotolia.com

www.ingramcontent.com/pod-product-compliance
Lightning Source LLC
Chambersburg PA
CBHW071016200526
45171CB00007B/241